YOUTH BIBLE

Tough Times

Youth Bible Study Guides

Sexuality

Following God

Image and Self-Esteem

Peer Pressure

Father God

Jesus Christ and the Holy Spirit

Sin, Forgiveness and Eternal Life

Church, Prayer and Worship

Sharing Your Faith

Tough Times

Money and Giving

Hunger, Poverty and Justice

YOUTH BIBLE STUDY GUIDE

Tough Times

COMPILED AND WRITTEN BY
CHIP AND HELEN KENDALL

Authentic

First published 2014 by Authentic Media Ltd
Presley Way, Crownhill, Milton Keynes, MK8 0ES.
www.authenticmedia.co.uk

British Library Cataloguing in Publication Data
A catalogue record for this book is available from the British Library

ISBN-13: 978-1-86024-637-1

Extracts taken from:
Eric Gaudion, *Braving the Storm*, Authentic, 2007
Sharon Witt, *Teen Talk*, Authentic, 2011
Andy Flannagan, *God 360°*, Spring Harvest and Authentic, 2006
Jess Wilson, *The Cutting Edge*, Authentic, 2008
John Lockley, *A Practical Workbook for the Depressed Christian*, Authentic, 2002
Ems Hancock and Ian Henderson, *Sorted*, Spring Harvest and Authentic, 2004

Cover and page design by Temple Design
Cover based on a design by Beth Ellis
Printed in Great Britain by Bell and Bain, Glasgow

Remember, I am very sad, and I have no home.

Remember the bitter poison that you gave me.

I remember well all my troubles, and I am very sad.

But then I think about this, and I have hope:

We are still alive because the LORD's faithful love never ends.

Every morning he shows it in new ways!

You are so very true and loyal!

I say to myself, 'The LORD is my God, and I trust him.'

(Lamentations 3:19–24)

Chip and Helen Kendall are Creative Arts Pastors at Audacious Church, Manchester, and also love spending as much time as possible with their kids, Cole, Eden and Elliot. They currently reside in Stockport, England and they still have trouble understanding each other's accents.

Chip tours the world, fronting the Chip Kendall Band. His album *Holy Freaks* and first book *The Mind of chipK: Enter at Your Own Risk* have helped loads of young people grow in their faith. He's also the driving force behind a new youth media movement called MYvoice with Cross Rhythms, as well as being a regular presenter on GodTV. All of these jobs continue to pave the way for him to speak at events everywhere. www.chipkendall.com

After working for ten years as a dancer and tour/bookings manager, Helen now juggles looking after the kids with her work at Audacious Church helping to develop dance and all things creative. She also enjoys doing some writing and project management. Helen loves the variety in her life, and no two days are ever the same.

Thank Yous

Massive thanks to Malcolm Down, Liz Williams and the rest of the gang at Authentic Media for giving us the opportunity to work on these study guides . . . it's been a blast. Thanks to everyone at Audacious Church for being an amazing church family. Thanks to lovely Lucy West for the fantastic photos. To everyone who talked to Chip for the 'people clips', thanks for your honesty and willingness to put up with the quirky questions. A really huge thank you to Brian and Norma Wilson for their 'hidden pearls' of wisdom. We loved your perspective on things. Finally, big thanks to all the authors whose work we have used in this book. You are an inspiration.

CONTENTS

INSTRUCTIONS

The book you're holding in your hands is a study guide. It's a compilation of extracts from lots of other books written about this subject. It might not make you the world's expert on the subject, but it should give you lots of useful information and, even better, it should give you some idea of what the Bible has to say about . . . TOUGH TIMES.

What is a 'reaction box'?

Throughout the book, you'll find these helpful little reaction boxes. We've added them so that you can decide for yourself what you think about what you've just read. Here's what one should look like once you've filled it in:

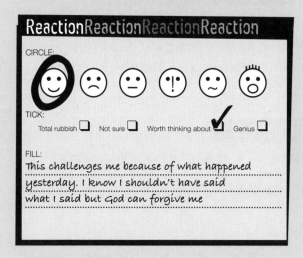

Pretty simple really . . .

Circle the face that reflects how you feel about it.

Tick the box that shows what you think about it.

Fill in any thoughts you have about what you've learned on the lines provided.

What are 'people clips'?

Just so you don't get too bored, we've added a bunch of 'people clips' to each study guide. These are people just like you, who were happy for us to pick their brains about various related topics. Who knows? Maybe you'll find someone you recognize.

What are 'hidden pearls'?

Everyone needs some good old-fashioned 'grandparently' advice, so we collected some pearls of wisdom from our friends Brian and Norma Wilson, which you can find scattered throughout the book.

What is a 'reality check'?

Finally, throughout the book you will come across sections called 'reality check'. These should provide a chance for you to apply what you've been learning to your own life experiences.

Other than that, the only rule that applies when reading this book is that you HAVE FUN! So start reading.

Chip & Helen

Introduction

STRENGTH IN WEAKNESS

God's kingdom is full of opposites. The last shall be first; the first shall be last. The humble shall be exalted; the proud shall be humiliated. But one of the most intriguing paradoxes is the verse that says God's power is most evident when we are at our weakest.

But the Lord said, 'My grace is all you need. Only when you are weak can everything be done completely by my power.' So I will gladly boast about my weaknesses. Then Christ's power can stay in me.

(2 Corinthians 12:9)

All followers of Christ will face seasons of suffering for one reason or another. Jesus promised that if the people of this world hated him, then they'll certainly hate us for being believers in him. Many Christians struggle with bouts of depression. It may be a physical diagnosis or a spiritual battle. The devil is a thief whose purpose is to steal our joy, kill our dreams and destroy our faith – 24 hours a day, 7 days a week . . . no lunch breaks either!

IF WE'RE GOING TO WEATHER LIFE'S TOUGHEST STORMS, WE MUST DIG DEEP and discover some of the amazing truths found only in God's word. In this book, we're not setting out to try and prove that Christians should be the saddest people alive. Neither are we making any attempts to tell people struggling with problems such as depression to simply 'get over it'.

Life is hard. And the Bible offers a lot of wisdom to help us not only cope, but make it through to the other side with a renewed sense of purpose and belonging.

So let's take a look at what the Bible says about . . . TOUGH TIMES.

what does the Bible say about TOUGH TIMES?

Suffering

'Come to me all of you who are tired from the heavy burden you have been forced to carry. I will give you rest. Accept my teaching. Learn from me. I am gentle and humble in spirit. And you will be able to get some rest. Yes, the teaching that I ask you to accept is easy. The load I give you to carry is light.'

(Matthew 11:28–30)

1

First up

Christians love to talk about 'passion'. We're *passionate* about God. We're *passionate* about life. We're *passionate* about seeing our unsaved friends turn to Christ, so that they too might experience this same *passion* that is inside us. But you don't hear many of us talking about 'suffering'. In light of this, it's interesting to note that the Latin root for the word passion — *'passio'* — literally means 'to suffer'! That's because the way to know if you're truly passionate about something is to ask yourself, 'How much am I really willing to suffer for this?'

For whatever reason, we will all face seasons in our lives when we suffer with something without really knowing why. Things like loneliness, bullying, the loss of a loved one, a prolonged illness, or any number of other injustices. Many of us will even suffer for being followers of Christ, and we may not even see much fruit from our persecution. It's important for us to remember that even in the worst of our toughest times, God is still faithful. He hasn't forgotten us, and he will keep his promises to us. He's close to the broken-hearted. Jesus himself knows what it means to suffer for no fault of his own.

As you read this first Life Lesson, you may identify with what you're reading and think, 'Wow, this is exactly how I'm feeling!' Or you may not. Maybe you'll think of people you know who are facing some of these struggles. If so, feel free to take a minute to pray for them. The Bible says that if one part of Christ's body (the Church) suffers, then the rest suffer with it. Let's be willing to stand in the gap and pray for our brothers and sisters all over the world who suffer day in and day out with this kind of stuff. After all, you may find yourself in their shoes one day, and wouldn't you want them praying for you?

What's the Point Of PAIN?

A bit like finding the reason for the existence of wasps and mosquitoes, it can be hard to discern a purpose behind the creation of pain, as it causes us so much unhappiness. Yet, pain serves us in ways that we don't always fully appreciate. Pain serves as a warning bell that something is wrong and needs to be fixed.

The whole point of physical exercise, so we are told, is to stretch the body beyond its normal limits so that it grows and develops in ways not previously possible. No pain, no gain. Apparently muscles get stronger by being pushed further than their pain barrier. When they recover, the increased blood flow and tissue activity actually leads to stronger muscles. Without the pain of being pushed, there would be no gain of growth and strengthening.

THE FACT IS GOD SOMETIMES ALLOWS PAIN IN OUR LIVES IN ORDER TO GAIN OUR ATTENTION. Now don't get me wrong here – I really wish there was another way! Yet when I read the Bible I discover that this has always been the case. Joseph found God's will for his life during his years in prison. Daniel proved God's love in a den of lions. Even the apostle Paul was thinking of this when he coined the well-known phrase, 'It is when I am weak that I am really strong' (2 Corinthians 12:10).

On the scale of pain of various kinds, the pain of bereavement is possibly one of the worst known to man. It's not physical pain, though it can sometimes feel so, yet it is very real. The phrase, 'Better to have loved and lost than never to have loved at all,' can seem very stark, even unkind, when one is suffering the pain of grief. Yet it reflects an aspect of human pain that is sometimes overlooked. **PAIN IS PART OF THE PRICE OF LOVING AND BEING LOVED.** Nowhere is that fact more starkly and powerfully portrayed than in Mel Gibson's film *The Passion of the Christ*. The very fact that the cruel death of Jesus is called his 'passion' gives a clue to this mysterious truth – that there is a price to pay for true love. God loved his world – our world – so much that unbelievable pain was a price he thought worth paying. 'He gave his only Son, so that everyone who believes in him would not be lost but have eternal life' (John 3:16).

Is it possible then, that some pain could actually be a gift from a loving God? 'Yet it was the LORD's will to crush him and cause him to suffer' (Isaiah 53:10, NIV). Not that we should look for pain in some masochistic kind of way but, rather, recognize that being in pain does not mean that God has forsaken us. Far from disqualifying us from the attention of the Lord, pain qualifies us for his loving care and support.

It's hard to see at the time, of course, but remembering that *nothing* that happens to us is pointless, can remove the sense of hopelessness we feel when we are long-term sufferers, and give us strong hope even in the middle of our pain.

Eric Gaudion, *Braving the Storm*, Authentic Media, 2007

ReactionReactionReactionReaction

CIRCLE:

TICK:
Total rubbish ☐ Not sure ☐ Worth thinking about ☐ Genius ☐

FILL:

....

....

....

....

Name: **Lucy Jayne Wells**

Age: **22**

Town: **Atlanta/ Manchester**

Occupation: **Dancer and choreographer**

If the world were square, what would the four corners of the earth be?

The four corners would be: Bering Strait (off the coast of Alaska), Chatham Islands (off the coast of New Zealand), Cape Horn, and Queen Elizabeth Islands.

Why did the chicken cross the road?

Because KFC was on the same side he was on!

What was your biggest childhood fear?

Probably spiders. Hated them! Actually, I still do! I've been known to start screaming and hitting myself if I thought one was on me.

In your opinion, why is there suffering in the world?

I believe there is suffering in the world because of sin. Even though we are a fallen world, and there are bad things that happen as a result of that, God hasn't left us alone. He continues to show us truth, and life, and points us to him. Because of the evil in the world, he sent his son Jesus to die on the cross for our sins, so that we could have eternal life. I heard something the other day which is so amazing: 'God has not stepped away from fallen creation, but has stepped into it by becoming Jesus. God works within the fallen world to effect change and he uses fallen people to accomplish his will.'

Dealing with Bullying

When most of us think of bullying, we immediately think of being backed into a corner of a classroom when the teacher is out of the room; being either verbally threatened or actually physically assaulted.

I remember as a Year 7 student, new to my secondary school, being locked in the store cupboard of the classroom by a tall fellow student. That was just because I was the new girl and she didn't really like me.

But in fact, whilst physical bullying does still unfortunately occur, it is the emotional type of bullying that can be just as hurtful and can stay with young people well into their adult lives and beyond.

Examples of bullying:

- **Physically hitting, punching or shoving another person, intentionally**
- **Name calling**
- **Deliberately provoking someone, making fun of them**
- **Encouraging someone to do something they do not want to do**
- **Excluding someone from your activities**
- **Gossiping**
- **Writing hurtful or nasty emails, letters or text messages**

I once saw a woman on an American talk show – then in her late thirties – complaining that she could not move forward in her life. She explained how she had suffered immense emotional and verbal bullying twenty years before.

The culprit had been a fellow female student at her school. The victim had become pregnant as a teenager and suffered a great deal of verbal abuse by other girls and one 'popular and attractive' girl in particular. Both women were reunited on the show in front of a studio audience.

The victim was still, to that day, absolutely devastated by the childhood bullying.

JUST SAY NO TO BULLIES

She had carried around a burden of rejection and hurt for two decades. The most frightening thing was the reaction of the alleged bully. She claimed she had no recollection of the girl or of the verbal attacks she had made. She apologized but remained incredulous at the degree of hurt she had caused.

Bully Busters

Ignore your bully

Bullies actually get their power from you, only if you give it away. Every time you react, you give the bully the result they were after. IGNORING SOMEONE TAKES AWAY ALL THEIR BULLY POWER and it all comes back to you!

Say 'NO!'

As soon as you say this single, powerful word, you are letting the bully know loud and clear that what they are doing or saying is not OK. If you struggle a bit with this at first, start by saying it under your breath or in your mind until you have the courage to say it out loud and with authority. You are worth it! Saying 'No!' loud and clear also lets everyone else around you know that what is happening is not OK. They are a witness to what is happening and your desire for it not to happen again.

Get help

If you are at school, it is really important that you let a teacher know as soon as you are the victim of a bully. Most schools have in place (or should do) very strict anti-bullying policies. If you cannot talk to your teacher, ask a friend to go on your behalf or to go with you.

Talk to your parents. They will deal with this on your behalf, and can talk to your teacher or head teacher. If you are in the workplace, bullying of any kind should also be against the rules. Tell your boss what is happening to you; they must act on this information. There have been many reported cases of severe injury due to workplace pranks or bullying, so never put up with it. You are worth way more than that!

Stand tall and have confidence

Bullies are looking for someone from whom they can steal confidence. Try and remember that **A BULLY IS REALLY JUST SOMEONE WHO IS LACKING CONFIDENCE IN THEMSELVES**. A bully tries to make others feel inferior to hide their own insecurities. When you remember this, you realize the bully is just a person who lacks confidence.

Don't look the other way if you see someone being bullied

If you see a friend or someone else being bullied, you owe it to them to let someone know, or step in for them. Make sure you do not get involved with a situation of physical bullying; instead, call for assistance. Looking the other way and ignoring a bullying situation is just as bad as being the bully yourself.

Sharon Witt, *Teen Talk*, Authentic Media, 2011

ReactionReactionReactionReaction

CIRCLE:

TICK:

Total rubbish ☐   Not sure ☐   Worth thinking about ☐   Genius ☐

FILL:

....

....

....

....

Everybody Needs Somebody

In the book *Bono on Bono*, there is a great quote from the man himself that says 'WEAKNESS DRIVES US TO FRIENDSHIPS'. Stop and think about that for a second. It pops up as he discusses how his lack of detailed musical knowledge means that he sometimes needs band-mate The Edge to paint the chords around a melody. Bono, however, is the stronger at dreaming up melodies from scratch. Together they make an amazing team, as their multi-million album sales testify, filling the gaps in each other's skill sets. Weakness drives them to friendship. It got me thinking that perhaps this is why we need friends.

Then my friend Lucy pointed out that God noted man's loneliness before the fall ('Then the LORD God said, 'I see that it is not good for the man to be alone. I will make the companion he needs, one just right for him' Genesis 2:18), suggesting that it is not simply our weaknesses that drive us to need friendship – somehow patching each other's holes – but a God-given need for others to share life with. It's the way he intended life to be.

My further thought, on reflection, was that perhaps weakness is actually part of perfection. I'll leave you to wrestle with that one.

Who are you happy to admit that you need in your life? We often struggle to admit this in our desire to be self-sufficient. **IT IS NOT FAILURE TO NEED PEOPLE. IT IS HUMAN.** No man is an island, it has been said. So why do we spend so much time chopping down the bridges that people build towards us? Ultimate success in this society is perceived as having your own car, your own house, your own plasma TV, etc., as this gives you the maximum amount of control possible. Rather than living on your own, isn't it really healthier to be living with someone else, even if it means sacrificing some 'freedom'? Solo living (which is still possible to sneakily do in the midst of something that looks like community) almost inevitably breeds selfishness and tunnel vision.

Spend some time in prayer thanking God for those who you 'need' in your life, and ask God to re-orientate your life away from self-sufficiency.

At this point, could you now tell your friends that you need them?

Andy Flannagan, *God 360°*, Spring Harvest and Authentic Media, 2006

Reaction Reaction Reaction Reaction

CIRCLE:

TICK:

Total rubbish ☐   Not sure ☐   Worth thinking about ☐   Genius ☐

FILL:

....

....

....

....

Suffering for Your Faith?

Helen Talks

Do bad things happen to Christians?

We are in touch with God, the creator of the universe, right? He can raise the dead and part the sea, so surely he can look after us and keep us safe from harm and suffering, can't he? If you've been a Christian for any length of time you've probably realized that while God could theoretically make life a fairytale dream for you to float through, it might not be what he chooses to do. Christians suffer for loads of different reasons – some that we can understand and some that we can't. Christians die of cancer, have their stuff nicked, have car crashes, go bankrupt and get bullied just like everyone else, and it's sometimes hard to figure out why God doesn't intervene.

F or some people, just becoming a Christian puts them very much in harm's way. On the whole we don't suffer major persecution for our faith in this country. While being a Christian isn't necessarily cool or popular, it's certainly not illegal and you are unlikely to get thrown in prison or killed for your faith. Here is a story from Emma Worrall at Open Doors, an organization that stands up for Christians who choose every day to stand up for their faith, whatever it costs.

Aziz is from Central Asia. He became a Christian as a teenager. Even though facing pressure from his parents, he has grown strong in his faith and is now responsible for at least seven cell groups.

'Six months after I became a Christian my mum was getting fed up and told me repeatedly to leave the church. She said, "You have a choice: your Jesus or your home. Are you going to give up your faith?" I told my parents I couldn't give up my faith. They started to beat me and threw me out of the house. I was 15 years old.'

Every day, persecuted Christians, like Aziz, have tough choices to make – to give up their faith in Jesus and have an easier life or to stand up for their faith and face losing everything. There might be times in your life when you, too, will have to choose to stand up for your faith; to choose between Jesus and your culture and even people close to you. The Bible calls you to stand up, and persecuted Christians give you the hope that you can stand up in the face of your culture.

You may not have had your life threatened for being a Christian, or have been kicked out of home, but maybe you face bullying and ridicule at school. Maybe your parents don't agree with your beliefs, and maybe you've even been threatened with violence. There is no precedent in the Bible that says that God will magically make these situations go away. Many of Jesus' closest friends, the disciples, were killed for their faith or had to flee their homes and families. **ALL WE CAN BE SURE OF IS THAT GOD WILL NEVER ABANDON US** and that he is no man's debtor. You can't give up more than he can give back.

'Everyone who has left houses, brothers, sisters, father, mother, children or farms to follow me will get much more than they left. And they will have eternal life.'
(Matthew 19:29)

That's basically saying that God will bring back to you everything you have lost and given up x 100! While that is amazing for the future, it doesn't lessen what you are going through right now. But remember that Jesus went through it too and in suffering for his gospel you are getting a glimpse of what it really feels like to be like Jesus.

ReactionReactionReactionReaction

CIRCLE:

😊 🙁 😐 ❗ 😕 😮

TICK:

Total rubbish ☐   Not sure ☐   Worth thinking about ☐   Genius ☐

FILL:

....

....

....

....

Hidden pearls

We pray for the persecuted
Christians that their
persecutors will be changed,
and also that those suffering
will be able to stand it.

I'm a Christian

You trust in the LORD for protection. You have made God Most High your place of safety. So nothing bad will happen to you. No diseases will come near your home. He will command his angels to protect you wherever you go. Their hands will catch you so that you will not hit your foot on a rock.

(Psalm 91:9–12)

O ften people think that becoming a Christian means that we'll somehow be protected from pain and sadness. And reading this psalm seems to confirm that. But, of course, we do get hurt. So what does this psalm mean?

Psalm 91 encourages us, God's people, to live by faith and not by fear. He promises to protect his people if they trust in him. And it's not just the psalmist who speaks – in verses 14–16 God himself speaks.

But why do Christians suffer? Why doesn't God deliver his people from harm? What good is a promise that doesn't seem to be kept? *What* is promised and *how* is it kept?

In actual fact, if we study the psalm closely, we see that **GOD DOESN'T PROMISE HIS PEOPLE THAT THERE WON'T BE TROUBLE**. What he states is that he'll go through the trials with them and that they will be ultimately delivered from them. God's people won't be touched by the rebellious acts that are committed against them. God won't punish his own people. They will see the rebellious judged, but they won't be judged as well – God's people will come through it.

It is vital that we know our Bibles well so that we know what the promises of God actually are. And God

So Why is This Happening to Me?

has kept his promise: by raising his one and only Son, Jesus, from the dead. It was the psalm that Satan misquoted to Jesus when he was tempted in the desert. We often read the Bible and are so quick to say 'It's me!' but we must understand that **THE BIBLE IS MORE THAN THAT: IT IS A REVELATION OF GOD HIMSELF.** This psalm is pointing to more hope in the New Testament – a lasting hope, an everlasting hope, the hope of eternal life.

God has promised to protect us if we trust in Jesus. He will do for us what he has done for his Son. We won't be judged as rebels on the last day. We have the hope of verse 13 to hold on to: 'You will have power to trample on lions and poisonous snakes.'

Jess Wilson, *The Cutting Edge*, Authentic Media, 2008

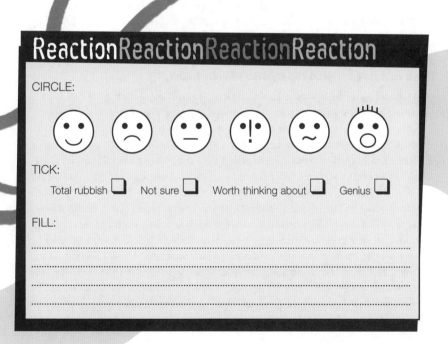

ReactionReactionReactionReaction

CIRCLE:

TICK:

Total rubbish ☐   Not sure ☐   Worth thinking about ☐   Genius ☐

FILL:

SAM'S Story

Chip talks

I recently chatted to a friend of mine who had a really bad accident and asked him about the experience . . .

Tell us briefly about your accident.

I was riding a motorbike on the way to work, when a 7.5-ton truck ploughed into me, knocking me off my bike. The truck then parked on my legs. I was trapped for 20 minutes until the fire service managed to lift the truck up with air bags and free me. At the hospital, I found out that my legs weren't badly broken, and only one leg had damage to the skin and muscle. The doctors were, however, concerned about the dangerously low levels of oxygen in my body. Later that evening, I stopped breathing and I had to be resuscitated. They didn't think I'd survive, but I did. I was then told by a specialist doctor that I would lose my left leg as the blood flow to my foot was so poor. After prayer, the blood flow had significantly improved. I then had surgery to have some skin removed and some muscle, followed by some skin grafts, which meant that I could keep my leg. I was in hospital for almost three months.

As a Christian, what did this do to your faith?

At first, my faith was a little shaken. I still loved God and I didn't blame him for what happened, nor did I blame the truck driver, but I wanted to know why God had allowed this to happen? Why did my loved ones have to suffer so much? Why me? When I was in hospital, despite the unanswered questions, I had a chance to read nearly the entire Bible as well as tell other patients and medical staff about God. I didn't get the chance to go to church for weeks, but the first chance I had, I went to the hospital chapel. When I was there, I just broke down in the middle of the service and wept with joy as I realized how much God had done for me and how he demonstrated his love for me when I was in the darkest place I could ever find myself. A few months later I realized that the situation had changed my life and the lives of loads more people for the better, and I am so grateful for that. Even through my family's suffering, they found peace, comfort, joy, and a relationship with God.

What advice would you give someone in a similar situation?

- Firstly, the way you're feeling now will pass. Things will get easier.

- Secondly, even though you are suffering, people around you are suffering just as much, but in a different way. Try and make yourself aware of your attitude to those who are supporting you. It is a journey you are all taking together!

- Thirdly, it's OK to be angry at God, and it's OK to have questions. But remember, regardless of what has happened he still loves you unconditionally. So make sure you have people around you to support you in your relationship with God.

- Fourthly, read the Bible, particularly the parts that are relevant to the situation you are in.

- Finally, don't give up hope. I'd given up hope that there would be good days again. Then God did some amazing healing within my body. So keep on praying!

Jesus came near to the city of Jericho. There was a blind man sitting beside the road. He was begging people for money. When he heard the people coming down the road, he asked, 'What is happening?' They told him, 'Jesus, the one from Nazareth, is coming here.' The blind man was excited and said, 'Jesus, Son of David, please help me!' The people who were in front leading the group criticized the blind man. They told him to be quiet. But he shouted more and more, 'Son of David, please help me!' Jesus stopped there and said, 'Bring that man to me!' When he came close, Jesus asked him, 'What do you want me to do for you?' He said, 'Lord, I want to see again.' Jesus said to him, 'You can see now. You are healed because you believed.' Then the man was able to see. He followed Jesus, thanking God. Everyone who saw this praised God for what happened.

(Luke 18:35–43)

History Has No Favourites

Imagine the accident and emergency department of your local hospital. This is a place of genuine apprehension for people. It is also a place of great 'levelling', in that there will be people waiting to be treated from every background, religion and age group.

Read Ecclesiastes 9:1–12.

T he journey through Ecclesiastes is like a plane ride. You get a sense that in chapter 9, after all the turbulence of the early chapters, we are just beginning to level out, and our stomachs are just starting to return from the upper reaches of our chest cavities. We definitely haven't landed yet, however.

Somewhere deep down, we still believe that because we belong to God, we should expect a slightly easier passage through this life. There are a number of subtle influences that have fed this lie throughout our lives, resulting in a default 'gut feeling' that it is the case. This is even though there is next to no biblical foundation for such a way of thinking. I think what we experience is a form of 'projection'. It's what we'd like to think, and we therefore project our preferred world-view onto the truth of how things are. However there is a definite absence of such rose-tinted glasses in chapter 9. We are encountering bright white truth, even if it hurts our eyes slightly.

In Matthew 5, either Jesus is doing an Ian McCaskill impression, and making a purely meteorological point, or he is adding his considerable weight to those words from Ecclesiastes, **'HE LETS THE SUN RISE FOR ALL PEOPLE, WHETHER THEY ARE GOOD OR BAD. HE SENDS RAIN TO THOSE WHO DO RIGHT AND TO THOSE WHO DO WRONG'** (Matthew 5:45). This is the sort of thing that it is enormously helpful to sort out in our heads and hearts before the tough times appear, but even this provides no immunity. Some perspective helps, because if this line of thinking is true, then it could be regarded as a bit of a bum deal if this life was all that there is. But it's not. These seventy or eighty years are like the hours of painful labour before the decades of joy.

Spend some time praying for the people in the A & E waiting room, and ask God for the grace to react well to the 'trials' of our lives, so the next time we are in that waiting room (real or virtual) of apprehension, we can know that it's not a moment where God is absent.

> My brothers and sisters, you will have many kinds of trouble. But this gives you a reason to be very happy. You know that when your faith is tested, you learn to be patient in suffering. If you let that patience work in you, the end result will be good. You will be mature and complete. You will be all that God wants you to be.

(James 1:2–4)

Andy Flannagan, *God 360°*, Spring Harvest and Authentic Media, 2006

ReactionReactionReactionReaction

CIRCLE:

☺ ☹ 😐 😮 😕 😲

TICK:

Total rubbish ☐   Not sure ☐   Worth thinking about ☐   Genius ☐

FILL:

....

....

....

....

Reality Check

I DON'T HEAR NO FAT LADY!

As long as there is still breath in your lungs, God still has a purpose for you here on this earth. You are alive and you are destined for great things, and the devil knows it. If you or someone you know is going through a season of suffering, just remember that old saying, 'It ain't over till the fat lady sings.' You're not dead yet. The character Job in the Bible suffered so many terrible things from Satan, but Satan wasn't permitted to take his life. And the same applies to so many of us today. So feel free to remind the devil: 'I don't hear no fat lady!'

Take a moment to write down any major issues or situations that are causing you to suffer right now:

....

....

....

....

....

Now think about the bigger picture. What are some of the lessons you are learning as you face these tough times? How might they be useful to you or God in the future (if at all)?

....

....

....

....

....

And finally, what response to these trials will you choose to have in order to show the devil he hasn't won?

....

....

....

....

....

Depression

He has sent me to comfort those who are sad, those in Zion who mourn. I will take away the ashes on their head, and I will give them a crown. I will take away their sadness, and I will give them the oil of happiness. I will take away their sorrow, and I will give them celebration clothes. He sent me to name them 'Good Trees' and 'The LORD's Wonderful Plant'.

(Isaiah 61:2–3)

√2

First up

Depression is a topic neither of us claim to be an expert in. We've both got close friends who either struggle with depression themselves or have family members suffering from depression. It's something even Christians are susceptible to, and seems to be increasingly prevalent among young people.

But what can we learn from the Bible about this terrible condition? What is God's response to it? Check out Isaiah 61:3. How incredible that God literally swaps our sadness for his happiness. He can exchange our 'sorrow' for his 'celebration clothes'. You may feel like the lowest thing on earth, but regardless of your emotions or your physical state of mind he calls you a 'Good Tree', something he's planted himself in order to bring him glory. Other translations of the Bible call these Good Trees 'Oaks of Righteousness'. There are many unique qualities that separate the oak tree from most other trees. But generally speaking, it's pretty obvious that oak trees are incredibly strong and massive! Can you picture yourself like that? God does.

If you're specifically struggling with depression, then the excerpts in this next Life Lesson have been written with you in mind. We've searched far and wide, and this is some of the best advice we can find anywhere on this subject. Take the time to fill in the reaction boxes at the end of each segment and try to apply what you've read to your own situation. You'll only really get as much out of this as you put into it, so don't be afraid to genuinely go for it. It might be a good idea to talk to someone about the points raised in this chapter, and discuss together what some of your next steps might look like.

When You're Feeling Down

If you are feeling down for any length of time (e.g. two weeks or more), it is important that you seek help. Being a teen can be tough at the best of times and it is quite common to feel overwhelmed sometimes and unable to cope. These feelings, however, should not last more than a couple of days. If you consistently feel sad and hopeless about your situation, it is important that you ask for help.

Talk to your parents, teacher, friend, school counsellor, sister, brother, aunty or church/youth group leader. Tell them honestly how you are feeling.

Signs of depression

- **Feeling sad, hopeless**
- **Crying often for no apparent reason**
- **Feeling tired and exhausted all the time**
- **Extreme weight loss or weight gain**
- **Lack of motivation and feeling like you cannot be bothered**
- **Loss of interest in activities**
- **Feeling worried and anxious often**
- **Sleeping too much or feeling like you need to sleep all the time**
- **Turning to drugs/alcohol to cope with life**
- **Harming/cutting yourself**

If you experience two or three of these symptoms for more than a week or two, please seek help from an adult.

Sharon Witt, *Teen Talk*, **Authentic Media, 2011**

ReactionReactionReactionReaction

CIRCLE:

☺ ☹ 😐 😦 😕 😲

TICK:

Total rubbish ☐   Not sure ☐   Worth thinking about ☐   Genius ☐

FILL:

....

....

....

....

Hidden pearls

Our friend is suffering with depression at the moment. She used to be fine, used to walk around town without a care in the world. Then, after some problems with her home she started to really suffer with depression. We pray for her but it was a shock for us – it just shows it can happen to anyone.

The Depressed Christian

Being depressed is bad enough in itself, but being a depressed Christian is worse. A depressed Christian has a double burden. Not only is he depressed but he also feels guilty because, as a Christian, he feels he is supposed to be full of joy. Joy is one of the fruits of the Spirit. So what's wrong with your spiritual life if there's no joy?

ot only are you facing your own problems, but you also have to deal with criticism from your Christian and non-Christian friends. Your non-Christian friends will be saying (probably out loud), 'I thought you were supposed to lose your worries when you became a Christian.' Your Christian friends will be muttering that you can't truly be a Christian; that they can't put their trust in you because of your mental state; and what sort of a witness are you giving?

The sad thing is that the guilt that you feel is totally underserved. Yet this guilty feeling is probably harder to deal with than the depression itself. For a start, **IT MAKES YOU DOUBT THE VALIDITY OF YOUR CHRISTIAN LIFE AND EXPERIENCE**. Then you start asking yourself whether you really were a Christian in the first place. Maybe you weren't (you think) and God is angry with you? On this basis, the treatment ought to be to pray harder, read the Bible more, confess more, and be really penitent for your sins.

So you try it – and it doesn't work. You try harder. And it's like banging your head on a brick wall – nice when you stop! So you feel even worse. Maybe God is really angry with you for being so stupid. Alternatively, maybe you think you've committed the unforgiveable sin.

Whatever it is you are feeling, stop. None of it is correct, and **YOU'RE TRYING TO CHANGE THE WRONG THINGS**. Part of the problem is that you are exhausting yourself trying to change things that seem to be unchangeable: and they seem unchangeable mainly because you are attacking them from the wrong direction.

For most depressed Christians, the depression is not caused by their spiritual state. On the other hand, depression will certainly have a knock-on effect on your spiritual life . . . Relax! You *are* a Christian. You therefore have the kindest, most loving, most caring, most sensitive, most trustworthy Friend on your side. **HE IS REALLY THERE – AND HE'S NOT GOING TO LET GO OF YOU!** . . . There is one verse that should be engraved upon the heart of every depressed Christian:

> `'Christ died for us while we were still sinners, and by this God showed how much he loves us.'`

(Romans 5:8)

God loves you now, as you are. He does not love you for what you could become, nor for what you might have been, but as you are, now. He loves you unconditionally. He does not insist upon your prayers, your praise, your time, your money, your attention, your Bible study, or even your thoughts as a condition before he is prepared to love you. **HE LOVES YOU AS YOU ARE**.

Yes, of course he looks forward to the day when you will be happier, when you will feel closer to him, when you will feel that your prayers are 'getting through', when you want to pray or read your Bible. But that day may well be some time away yet and God has his own good reasons for allowing your depression. Meanwhile, he loves you unconditionally, whether you are aware of it or not.

John Lockley, *A Practical Workbook for the Depressed Christian*, Authentic Media, 2002

ReactionReactionReactionReaction

CIRCLE:

TICK:

Total rubbish ☐   Not sure ☐   Worth thinking about ☐   Genius ☐

FILL:

....

....

....

....

Name: **Bethan Oakley**

Age: **18**

Town: **Crewe**

Occupation: **Student**

What are you studying?

A-levels in psychology, English literature and drama.

What do you do when you arrive at a party and another girl is wearing the same thing as you?

Laugh nervously and try to make some kind of joke out of it so it's not so embarrassing.

Which number gets dialled the most on your phone?

Either my boyfriend or my mum.

What was your best Christmas present last year?

Tickets to see the West End show Les Misérables.

Can a Christian be depressed?

Oh yeah, definitely. But I think that topic is a bit taboo. If a Christian is made to feel as though they're not allowed to be depressed, they won't admit to it. Then they don't feel very spiritual and that just makes them feel worse.

Is there a solution?

Yes, I think there is. Some Christians would say just prayer. But I don't think it's wrong to take anti-depressants, or to go for counselling, even from a secular counsellor.

Stress

There is no doubt that being a teen can be a very stressful time.
You are coping with huge changes including:

- **School/homework pressures**
- **Body changes**
- **Physical changes**
- **Emotions**
- **Parents**
- **Friendships**

It is really important that you find healthy outlets for dealing with any stress
that you are feeling. Some people deal with stress by exercising or talking with
friends. Make sure you find the outlet that best suits you, and make sure you
take action.

One of the biggest stress indicators is illness, so make sure you take stress
seriously and keep a healthy check on yourself.

Stress Indicators

- **Inability to sleep properly**
- **Not being able to eat – disinterest in food**
- **Lack of interest in friends and things that you usually enjoy doing**
- **Crying often or feeling down in the dumps**
- **A feeling of being unable to cope**

If you have been struggling with any of the above symptoms for a few weeks
or more, you could very well be struggling with stress. It is important that you
talk with your parents, teacher or school counsellor. It would also be good to
visit your local doctor to get a thorough examination.

Stress Busters

If you are feeling a bit stressed, try some of the following solutions:

- **Exercise**. This is great for relieving stress because when you exercise, your
  body releases its own natural 'feel good' chemicals. It also helps the blood
  flow better throughout your body, giving it a great boost.

- **Go for a long walk**. *(See previous)*

- **Have a couple of early nights**. If you are stressed, this could be a sign that your body needs a bit of a rest. Make yourself a warm milky drink, grab a good book and read for a little while before having a good, long sleep. You need between eight and ten hours sleep per night to feel well rested and stress-free. Make sleep your priority, and other things will fall into place.

- **Eat well**. Fill your body with lots of fruit and vegetables. This may sound a bit boring. However, spending a few days giving your body extra minerals and vitamins will help restore you.

- **Hire your favourite comedy movie** (or chick flick if you are a girl!) from the DVD store. Laughter also releases your body's natural endorphins that help to make you feel better.

- **Do something you love doing**, e.g. paint, draw, write, hike, ride, or make something. What is your passion?

- **Spend a day out with friends**. Go shopping, hang out together.

Sharon Witt, *Teen Talk*, Authentic Media, 2011

ReactionReactionReactionReaction

CIRCLE:

😊 ☹️ 😐 😣 😕 😲

TICK:

Total rubbish ☐ Not sure ☐ Worth thinking about ☐ Genius ☐

FILL:

....

....

....

....

Bin It to Win It 🗑

'So I tell you, don't worry about the things you need to live – what you will eat, drink or wear. Life is more than what you eat, and you are more than what you wear. Look at the birds. They don't plant, harvest or save food in barns, but your heavenly Father feeds them. Don't you know you are worth much more than they are? You cannot add any time to your life by worrying about it.

And why do you worry about clothes? Look at the wild flowers in the field. See how they grow. They don't work or make clothes for themselves. But I tell you that even Solomon, the great and rich king, was not dressed as beautifully as one of these flowers. If God makes what grows in the field so beautiful, what do you think he will do for you? It's just grass – one day it's alive, and the next day someone throws it into a fire. But God cares enough to make it beautiful. Surely he will do much more for you. Your faith is so small!

Don't worry and say, 'What will we eat?' or 'What will we drink?' or 'What will we wear?' That's what those people who don't know God are always thinking about. Don't worry, because your Father in heaven knows that you need all these things. Your first concern should always be God's kingdom and whatever he considers good and right. Then he will give you all these other things you need. So don't worry about tomorrow. Tomorrow will take care of itself. Each day has enough trouble of its own.'

(Matthew 6:25–34)

In this passage I hear echoes of Jesus' beautiful words to Martha in Luke 10:41–42: 'Martha, Martha, you are getting worried and upset about too many things. **ONLY ONE THING IS IMPORTANT**. Mary has made the right choice, and it will never be taken away from her.'

In Matthew 6 Jesus is simply listing the 'many things' that we worry about. Later in the chapter we find out what the 'one thing' that we should be worried about is. (I'm realizing how ironic it is that I just used that phrase. In our speech patterns we have actually normalized worrying.) The 'one thing' is: 'Your first concern should always be God's kingdom and whatever he considers good and right. Then he will give you all these other things you need.'

There is real power in simply listing your worries. By naming them you remove the subconscious power from them. Write them on a piece of paper and then go out for a walk. Don't immediately throw the paper into the nearest bin. Instead **TAKE SOME TIME TO LAY THESE WORRIES BEFORE GOD HONESTLY,** one at a time, and when you know that the time is right, just dump them in a roadside bin. They will be far from your house and you can experience the difference during your walk home, knowing that God has heard you and that you've been obedient to his command: 'Don't worry about the things you need to live.'

In the same way that peace is not simply the absence of war, you could also say that peace is not simply the absence of worry.

Let the peace that Christ gives control your thinking. It is for peace that you were chosen to be together in one body. And always be thankful.

(Colossians 3:15)

When do we truly let peace 'rule'? I think I'm happy to let peace in as a passenger every so often, when I need it, but what would my life look like if I let it drive? No more worrying about the speed cameras and short-sighted pedestrians of my emotional and spiritual world. Peace just slips down a gear and smiles reassuringly that he knows where he's going and that we'll make it on time.

Don't worry.

Andy Flannagan, *God 360°*, Spring Harvest and Authentic Media, 2006

ReactionReactionReactionReaction

CIRCLE:

TICK:

Total rubbish ☐   Not sure ☐   Worth thinking about ☐   Genius ☐

FILL:

....

....

Worry and Anxiety

Helen talks

We all go through times when we feel worried or anxious about things. For me it's often when I've taken on too much and then I start to feel overwhelmed and stressed about how I am going to do all the things I've committed to. While you are a teenager there are some pretty major pressures and things to worry about: exam results, career choices, relationships, trying to get a first job, decisions about the future. Not to mention other things like bullying, family problems, abusive relationships, issues of image and identity which can also cause anxiety and worry.

Do you feel like you are in control of your anxiety and worry, or is it something that dictates and controls how you live your life? For some people dealing with anxiety is a question of **MAKING A DECISION TO TRUST GOD AND NOT TO WORRY SO MUCH**, being disciplined to 'capture every thought and make it give up and obey Christ' (2 Corinthians 10:5). Learning and declaring verses in the Bible where we are told of God's love, provision and plan for our lives can also help.

For some people problems of anxiety can be a lot more serious and difficult to overcome. If you struggle with panic attacks, severe anxiety about social situations or about having to talk to new people, or have a serious phobia, it may be that you have some kind of anxiety disorder.

There are loads of different ways anxiety can express itself. It might be in obsessive behaviour, being overly worried about cleanliness, or having phobias about particular things – it could even have very physical symptoms. If this is you, then it's really important to get some professional help. As with depression, there can be stigma and guilt attached to having this kind of problem, but you shouldn't feel like you need to work it out on your own, or that you are less of a Christian if you need help. An anxiety disorder is an illness just like any other. If you had a broken leg, you wouldn't just pray – you'd go to the hospital too, right? For an anxiety problem you might need professional help as well as prayer and Bible verses.

There are lots of websites that can offer advice about dealing with anxiety problems but you can also talk to your GP or a counsellor about what kind of help would be best for you. The main thing is to take action. **GOD WANTS YOU WHOLE AND WELL IN MIND, BODY AND SPIRIT**, so you can live the life he has for you to the full. Don't waste time. Once you recognize that you have a problem, get help. Many people go for years struggling alone or not really acknowledging they have a problem. If you are concerned that you might have an anxiety disorder, then seek help getting a diagnosis and start to deal with the problem. God loves you so much and has a great plan for your life, but you might need to work through some issues in order to be able to live it to the full. He is with you all the way.

You might want to start by praying this prayer:

Dear Father, thank you for your love and acceptance. Thank you that I can come to you whole or broken and you will always have time for me and my worries. I bring my anxieties and fears to you now and ask that you help me to feel your peace. Please give me wisdom in seeking out help and bring the right people alongside me to help me work through this, so I can be fully ready to embrace the life you have for me.

Amen.

You may find the following verses helpful: Philippians 4:4–7, John 14:1,27; and 1 Peter 5:7.

ReactionReactionReactionReaction

CIRCLE:

TICK:

Total rubbish ☐   Not sure ☐   Worth thinking about ☐   Genius ☐

FILL:

....

....

Faith, Logic and Emotions

It is vital for Christians to understand that our emotions are not necessarily a good guide to what is going on, nor to what we should be doing in the next few minutes or hours. Unquestionably, this is where logic should apply first and foremost. For example, in the case of the person who is scared to do anything new, his emotions may be saying, 'Don't do this, it's the unknown, it's frightening – don't do it,' whereas his logic may be saying, 'This is an obvious and excellent opportunity to do something – grasp this opportunity immediately because you may not get another one like it for some time.'

Faith is often like this. The Bible talks about those who are tossed around by the wind in terms of faith; such people often depend entirely upon their emotional appreciation of God for the depth of their faith. When their emotions are in a state of upheaval their faith will be too, so at the time when they most need God they will feel as though he's not there!

There is a modern parable about this, of three tightrope walkers called Faith, Emotion and Logic. When Emotion went first along the wire with Faith and Logic following afterwards, Emotion got very worried, wavered, and fell off, dragging the other two down with him. On the other hand, when Logic went first with Faith second and Emotion bringing up the rear, everything was on a much more even keel. Emotion was steadied by the effects of the other two.

Caring for your emotions

Depression is in many ways a disease of the emotions, and getting the emotions back into line should be the prime target for any depressed person. It is important that we learn to laugh when we want to, to cry when we need to, to be joyful and to be sorrowful when appropriate. As Ecclesiastes says, there is a time for everything: **THERE IS A TIME TO CRY AND A TIME TO LAUGH;** there is a time to be joyful and there is a time to be sad.

Unfortunately, in depression the emotions are flattened and this is a characteristic sign of the disease. **NOT ONLY CAN YOU NOT BE HAPPY, YOU CAN'T BE VERY SAD EITHER**. It may well be that the mind is trying to avoid dealing with something that it finds intolerably sad – such as the threat of death or disease, or the loss of a loved one; the mind protects you from feeling unbearably despondent. Unfortunately, this is at the cost of not being able to show much emotion in any direction – which means that although you are not able to be too sad, you are not able to be too happy either.

Using your emotions properly

Our emotions need feeding and our emotions also need listening to. We need to respond to how we feel – not how we feel in terms of memories from what has gone on in the past, but from the emotion that we feel as a result of what is happening now. If something today is making you upset, then react to it. Display your anger (if it is justified and if it is righteous anger). Don't push it down and out of the way. If something today is making you feel sad, then let it out – cry. If something today is making you feel almost unbearably happy, then be prepared to laugh and dance and jump about and have a party to celebrate it. This is what I mean by feeding the emotions – reacting with appropriate emotions to today's events.

What I do not want you to do is dwell on the emotions that you have as a result of things that happened in the past. If there is no good reason for you to 'feel' sad today, it is not appropriate for you to go around expressing that sadness. Don't go and feed the emotions that are from yesterday or the day before, or maybe years ago – because these emotions should by now be dead and buried. **APPROPRIATE EMOTION SHOULD BE CONNECTED WITH THINGS THAT ARE HAPPENING NOW** rather than things that happened in the past. Feed today's emotions, express today's emotions, enjoy today's emotions – whether they are happy or sad. They will make living that much deeper and that much richer. God made emotions, and they're good for you.

John Lockley, *A Practical Workbook for the Depressed Christian*, Authentic Media, 2002

ReactionReactionReactionReaction

CIRCLE:

☺ ☹ 😐 ⁉️ 🙁 😲

TICK:

Total rubbish ☐   Not sure ☐   Worth thinking about ☐   Genius ☐

FILL:

....
....
....
....

How Do We Measure Our Worth?

How do you measure your worth? By your performance in school, university or at work? By the designer labels on the clothes you wear? By where you live or by how much money you or your family earn? Maybe by the people you socialize with? Do you constantly worry about being popular, and being accepted and loved by other people?

I've been prone to questioning my worth over the last few years. I have a hugely competitive streak in me, but rather than just a bit of healthy competition, I became obsessed with being the best at everything I did. I would measure my worth by so many different things, but here are my top five:

- **School achievements**
- **The way I looked when I got up/during the day/when I went out/when I went to bed**
- **How many friends I had**
- **The attention I received from boys**
- **Whether or not I was cutting myself**

I cared more about whether I'd met my own high standards than I did about what other people thought of me. Although other people's negative comments hurt, it is far easier to brush them off when you feel happy with yourself. In any case, I had more than enough problems trying to live up to my own unrealistically high expectations.

Naturally it was hard to always be the best at everything and if someone did better than me in an exam I would wonder why I'd done so badly. If I saw someone who was thinner or prettier than me, I'd hate myself, and if a friend was cruel to me **I WOULD BLAME MYSELF REGARDLESS OF WHOSE FAULT IT WAS.** If one of my friends received more attention from a guy than I did, then I would wonder what was wrong with me and then come to the conclusion that it was because I was ugly and fat. Most of these situations led to me cutting myself, which would be the beginning of a vicious circle: I would cut myself, then feel guilty about it, which in turn made me feel like a failure, so I'd despise myself and that would make me cut myself, and the whole thing would start again.

I can clearly remember the first time someone told me that I was in the middle of a vicious circle and that I had to break it. The key is to eliminate one of the factors, because without that factor the circle cannot continue. For me the main factor I needed to eliminate was the failure, as it had always been one of my biggest issues, and everything that I felt about myself stemmed from my feelings of failure. Obviously I couldn't stop feeling this way overnight; I had to train myself out of bad ways of thinking about myself. I won't pretend it was easy, and I still have days where I'm not keen on myself, but I've slowly learnt to be realistic and rational and to try and see things from God's perspective.

Self-worth is such a big thing in our daily lives and in our culture. Many of my friends also continually question their worth. Two of my close friends are dangerously bulimic – one of them since the age of 14. I've got friends who sleep around and ones who've regularly had to take morning-after pills after having unprotected sex. When we were 17 I supported one of my closest friends through a horrific abortion, although it went against my own personal beliefs. I've got friends who've dabbled with self-harm and those who drink excessive amounts of alcohol. I know so many people who dislike and even hate themselves, and **I DON'T THINK I KNOW ONE PERSON WHO DOESN'T HAVE THEIR OWN INSECURITIES.**

Say I stood in front of you with a £10 note in my hands. What's it worth? Ten pounds sterling, right? So what if I rip it in half? Sure, it's in two pieces now, but if I was to ask you what it is, you'd still say a £10 note; it's still worth ten pounds regardless of the condition that it is in. Well, we can relate that to how God sees us. My life certainly can't be compared to a crisp new £10 note. At times I've felt that everything I am has been systematically damaged and destroyed and ripped into so many pieces that I can never be whole again. So often our lives are not what God planned for us. Luckily for us, though, our worth in God's eyes does not change. He does not criticize or measure us against each other. In God's eyes, we are still the original crisp £10 note. Often when we compare ourselves unfavourably to others, we feel that we have nothing to contribute. But what does God's book have to say about worth?

A person's body has more than one part. It has many parts. The foot might say, 'I am not a hand, so I don't belong to the body.' But saying this would not stop the foot from being a part of the body ... If the whole body were an eye, it would not be able to hear ... But as it is, God put the parts in the body as he wanted them. He made a place for each one ... those parts of the body that seem to be weaker are actually very important.

(1 Corinthians 12:14–18,22)

This is such an important passage, as it not only teaches us about how we are all an integral part of God's plan, but also shows us why we shouldn't compare ourselves to each other. If everyone had the same talents and did the same job 'the body' wouldn't work. But God blessed us with different talents and gifts and we all have a place in his work and his plan. So instead of comparing ourselves to each other, we can trust that God has an awesome plan for our lives and that he will equip us with the tools that we will need.

'I have good plans for you. I don't plan to hurt you. I plan to give you hope and a good future.'

(Jeremiah 29:11)

Jess Wilson, *The Cutting Edge*, Authentic Media, 2008

ReactionReactionReactionReaction

CIRCLE:

TICK:

Total rubbish ☐   Not sure ☐   Worth thinking about ☐   Genius ☐

FILL:

....

....

....

....

Help is at Hand

As I write, I hear another story of teenagers taking their lives. The most upsetting thing about the tragic event was that the teens felt they had no other option and no one to talk to about what they were planning to do.

Suicide is final. Once a person succeeds with taking their life, there are no other options. All that is left behind is a string of unanswered questions, guilt and extreme distress for those who loved them.

When I was a teenager, one of my dearest friends decided that suicide was his only option. He was successful in removing himself from the world, but left behind a shattered community of family and friends. My personal anguish and pain regarding the loss of my friend lingered for many years.

You may feel that life is too hard and not worth continuing. But for most people, this is a stage you need to go through. Yes, it is extremely painful, and there's no denying that. Most people, however, find that they look back on such times and reflect, thankful that they did not take the most extreme and final measure of opting out of life.

If you are suicidal or really wanting to take a ticket out of life, it is so important that you **seek help immediately.** This may be easier said than done. Who do you tell? What if they do not take you seriously?

You can start by telling your parent, school counsellor, teacher or friend. The important thing is that you tell someone what you are going through. You are not crazy. You are just going through a tough time like many other people do.

Sharon Witt, *Teen Talk*, Authentic Media, 2011

ReactionReactionReactionReaction

CIRCLE:

TICK:

Total rubbish ☐　Not sure ☐　Worth thinking about ☐　Genius ☐

FILL:

....

....

Reality Check

IT'S ALWAYS DARKEST BEFORE THE DAWN

God has implemented some of the most incredibly profound truth into the most basic natural phenomena. A sunrise is beautiful in and of itself, but it can also become an incredible metaphor for the way God chooses to work in our lives.

At the end of this Life Lesson on the topic of depression, we thought it might be a good idea to give you this little mind journey to meditate on, then some space to write down your own thoughts and musings. Ask yourself, 'How does this relate to God moving in me?'

It's been a long, hard night. Raining off and on, extremely windy, noises coming from every direction making you feel quite scared. You've been up most of the night, tossing and turning in your bed, trying to cope with the deep sense of loneliness and uselessness that makes your heart ache to bursting point. Then, just when it couldn't possibly get any darker or colder, everything goes quiet. There's a moment of stillness that causes you to unconsciously hold your breath as the first rays of sunlight begin to appear on the horizon. As the day slowly begins to dawn, you feel undeniably warmer with each passing minute. Outside, the sky turns from dark black to deep red and eventually light blue. You close your eyes, and finally your soul is satisfied. Rest is sweet and your dreams quickly swallow you into sleep.

Solutions

The first step to becoming wise is to look for wisdom, so use everything you have to get understanding.

(Proverbs 4:7)

First up

'I may not have the answer, but I know Someone who does . . .'

Have you ever heard these words spoken in reply to life's tough questions? The Bible is the word of God. Jesus is God's word in human form. As such, we would be wise to always allow him to have the final word in our lives — especially when we face tough times.

This next Life Lesson simply highlights some of the promises we find in the verses of the Bible. We've tried to organize them in such a way that they can serve as a useful reference for you when you're up against serious hurdles of doubt, frustration, depression and anxiety. You may want to memorize the verses that speak loudest to your heart. This is probably one of the best ways of applying what God says to your own situation. Recite them aloud in the middle of your storm. Encourage others with them when they feel like giving up. None of us can truthfully claim to have all the solutions, but the Bible is 'like a lamp that guides [our] steps, [and] a light that shows the path [we] should take' (Psalm 119:105). So even on our darkest days we can treat it like one.

Promises

You must continue to follow the teaching you heard from the beginning. If you do that, you will always be in the Son and in the Father. And this is what the Son promised us – eternal life.
(1 John 2:24–25)

I am sure that the good work God began in you will continue until he completes it on the day when Jesus Christ comes again.
(Philippians 1:6)

But in all these troubles we have complete victory through God, who has shown his love for us. Yes, I am sure that nothing can separate us from God's love – not death or life, not angels or ruling spirits. I am sure that nothing now, nothing in the future, no powers, nothing above us or below us – nothing in the whole created world – will ever be able to separate us from the love God has shown us in Christ Jesus our Lord.
(Romans 8:37–39)

Jacob, the LORD created you. Israel, he made you, and now he says, 'Don't be afraid. I saved you. I named you. You are mine. When you have troubles, I am with you. When you cross rivers, you will not be hurt. When you walk through fire, you will not be burned; the flames will not hurt you.'
(Isaiah 43:1–2)

God is our protection and source of strength.
He is always ready to help us in times of trouble.
(Psalm 46:1)

'I have told you these things so that you can have peace in me.
In this world you will have troubles. But be brave! I have
defeated the world!'
(John 16:33)

So remember that the LORD your God is the only God, and you
can trust him! He keeps his agreement. He shows his love and
kindness to all people who love him and obey his commands. He
continues to show his love and kindness through a thousand
generations.
(Deuteronomy 7:9)

ReactionReactionReactionReaction

CIRCLE:

TICK:

Total rubbish ☐   Not sure ☐   Worth thinking about ☐   Genius ☐

FILL:

....

....

....

....

Emmanuel
God with Us

One of the most tricky (and valid) questions I regularly get asked is, 'How can a good God allow bad things to happen?' Often, the person asking this question is right in the middle of a horrible situation. Maybe a close relative has recently been diagnosed with a terminal illness or even died, or maybe they've just been dumped by their boyfriend or girlfriend. The question they're really asking is 'DOES GOD CARE?'

I believe that God is good, and that he cares for us more deeply than we could possibly begin to imagine. One of the names of God that we're shown in Scripture is 'Emmanuel' which is translated 'God with us'. Despite whatever heartache, pain or frustration we may face, God promises to be right there with us, every step of the way, even if we don't see him or feel him. Even if we don't believe in him, he is still 'God with us'.

This is the God who reveals himself as a loving parent.

The LORD is as kind to his followers, as a father is to his children.
(Psalm 103:13)

This is the God who reveals himself as Jesus, our constant Saviour.

Jesus is the one God honoured by giving him a place at his right side. He made him our Leader and Saviour.
(Acts 5:31a)

This is the God who reveals himself as the Holy Spirit, our comforter and helper.

'I will ask the Father, and he will give you another Helper to be with you forever. The Helper is the Spirit of truth.'
(John 14:16–17a)

If you believe that what the Bible says is true, then you can rest assured that no matter what you are facing in life, God cares for you. You are more valuable to him than you can possibly imagine. Jesus says it best in Matthew 10:29–31:

'When birds are sold, two small birds cost only a penny. But not even one of those little birds can die without your Father knowing it. God even knows how many hairs are on your head. So don't be afraid. You are worth more than a whole flock of birds.'

ReactionReactionReactionReaction

CIRCLE:

☺ ☹ 😐 😮 😕 😧

TICK:

Total rubbish ☐   Not sure ☐   Worth thinking about ☐   Genius ☐

FILL:

....

....

....

....

Seeing the End from the Beginning

Chip talks

At various points in my life, I've been blessed with significant moments of insight into the nature of God. On my wedding day, I cried my eyes out watching my beautiful bride walk down the aisle. For me, it was a brief glimpse into the heart and mind of Jesus, and how he sees the church as his Bride. Also, when my wife and I had our first child, I was able to finally know and experience for the first time a bit of the unconditional love the Father has for us his children. But no matter how much I think about it, I simply cannot get my head around other aspects of God's nature.

F or instance, how is God able to be everywhere all the time? He's out at the furthest reaches of the universe, and yet somehow he's also in my next-door neighbour's kitchen? That's pretty incredible. Or take for example his omniscience – his ability to know all things. God knows the exact thoughts of every single human being on the planet right now, at this precise moment. I don't think I could cope with knowing all the thoughts of just my family for more than about a minute. I'd probably have a nervous breakdown!

But one of the greatest mysteries for me, when it comes to understanding God's nature, is his ability to exist outside of time. He has no beginning and no end. He is the Alpha and the Omega. He sees the end from the beginning. **THAT'S INSANE! AND YET, IN A LOT OF WAYS IT'S EXTREMELY COMFORTING**. Why? Because I can always know beyond a shadow of a doubt that nothing takes God by surprise. Nothing fazes him. He's never up there in heaven wringing his hands and stressing out, thinking, 'Oh no, I hadn't anticipated that. What in the world am I going to do now?' He already knows how the story ends. After all, he wrote the book!

Sometimes the story God is telling through our lives doesn't make any sense to us at the time. If we were the ones telling it, there would be some serious alterations. But in these moments the best thing we can do is remember the words of Philippians 1:6:

I am sure that the good work God began in you will continue until he completes it on the day when Jesus Christ comes again.

God sees the end from the beginning.
It's his story, not ours, to tell.
And it's definitely going to be a good one.

Questions for you to consider:

- *What are some moments in your life when you've undoubtedly experienced something of the nature and heart of God?*

- *If you could rewrite the story of your life up until now, what would be your top 5 changes?*

- *What are the situations you're facing right now that you really need God to turn around for good?*

ReactionReactionReactionReaction

CIRCLE:

😊 😟 😐 😮 🙂 😲

TICK:

Total rubbish ☐   Not sure ☐   Worth thinking about ☐   Genius ☐

FILL:

....

....

....

....

Thanksgiving and Praise

Come through the gates to his Temple giving thanks to him.
Enter his courtyards with songs of praise.
Honour him and bless his name.
The LORD is good!
There is no end to his faithful love.
We can trust him for ever and ever!

(Psalm 100:4–5)

I am sad and hurting.
God, lift me up and save me!
I will praise God's name in song.
I will honour him by giving him thanks

(Psalm 69:29–30)

In the same way, the LORD will bless Zion. He will feel sorry
for her and her people, and he will do something great for her.
He will turn the desert into a garden. It will be like the
Garden of Eden. The land was empty, but it will become like the
LORD's garden. People there will be very happy. They will sing
victory songs to thank God for what he did.

(Isaiah 51:3)

Don't worry about anything, but pray and ask God for everything you need, always giving thanks for what you have. And because you belong to Christ Jesus, God's peace will stand guard over all your thoughts and feelings. His peace can do this far better than our human minds.

(Philippians 4:6–7)

My soul, praise the Lord!
    Every part of me, praise his holy name!
My soul, praise the Lord
    and never forget how kind he is!
He forgives all our sins
    and heals all our sicknesses.
He saves us from the grave,
    and he gives us love and compassion.
He gives us plenty of good things.
    He makes us young again,
    like an eagle that grows new feathers.

(Psalm 103:1–5)

ReactionReactionReactionReaction

CIRCLE:

☺ ☹ 😐 ‼ 😕 😲

TICK:

Total rubbish ☐   Not sure ☐   Worth thinking about ☐   Genius ☐

FILL:

....
....
....
....

Praising God Through Our Circumstances

Many people talk about 'praising God through our circumstances', which means praising God in everything that we do, even during the tough times when we feel him to be so far away. It's something that I've always had trouble understanding. Personally, I find it incredibly easy to thank God when things are going really well in my life – if I've passed a hard exam, I've met someone great or I've received some good news. As a general rule, I'm easily able to see God working in my life when things are going the right way. But when things happen in my life that I can't fix, that are beyond my control, which upset me and cause me pain, I find it very hard to praise God. Why would I feel like praising God when my life seems to be falling apart around me? I used to think, 'What a stupid thing to do! Surely if you can manage to praise God, then the situation you're in can't be that bad.' But I recently had an experience that made me change my mind.

At the moment, I'm a student at university and living in a huge city during my term times. I've been blessed with an amazing set of friends and barely a week goes by without me visiting one of them or someone coming to stay with me. Some time ago, one of my closest friends came to spend some time with me. Having been great friends from childhood we are very close, and she'd stayed with me plenty of times before. Sadly, this time was different. While she was staying with me, she was raped.

I was not with her at the time, and was horrified when I found out what had happened. I felt a mixture of anger, pain, fear and powerlessness. But the overriding feeling was the familiar one of failure and guilt. All I could think of was, 'What if . . .' What if I had been there . . . if she hadn't gone . . . if I had tried harder to persuade her not to meet him or refused to let her go and, above all . . . if she'd never come to see me. Although I wasn't the one who had subjected her to this ordeal, I still felt that it was somehow my fault.

A few months later, I found myself in floods of tears, sitting in the kitchen of my university accommodation in the dark, just staring out into the city. This was the city I had initially loved, but now, because of my friend's rape, had become a city I detested and was afraid to be in. I hated the fact that I was potentially sharing a city with a man who'd stolen something so precious from my close friend that she couldn't ever get back. It made me feel sick to just be there.

I sat in the dark staring at the city whose lights I had loved looking at, and wept: I wept for my friend and what had happened to her; I wept because of the anger I still felt; I wept because of the failure and guilt I had burdened myself with; and I wept because of the love I had lost for my life in that city.

Then I realized that although nothing would ever take away the cold hard fact that my friend had been raped there, **I WAS NOT WILLING TO GIVE HER ATTACKER CONTROL OVER MY FEELINGS AND ACTIONS** as well as hers. I wouldn't let him make me hate the city I had chosen to be in. It was at that moment that I felt I understood what it meant to praise God through our circumstances. Although I was hurting and my friend was hurting, I

remembered that God is God, regardless of any of us and what we are going through. God is God and I could praise him because I know my friend will be a stronger person after this experience, and because I honestly believe that God will use this situation for good, as it says in Romans 8:28:

> We know that in everything God works for the good of those who love him. These are the people God chose, because that was his plan.

I had always believed that 'praising God through our circumstances' had meant that we had to wipe our tears, jump up and down with our hands in the air, carefree, praising God . . . but I was wrong. We can praise God when we have tears streaming down our faces, and mascara running everywhere. We can praise God when we are doubtful and uncertain and when we are desperate, because **GOD IS GOD AND WE SHOULD PRAISE HIM SIMPLY FOR THAT**. God meets us where we are, whether our lives are going the way we want them to or not, or when our closest friend is raped and we don't know how we can stand to live in the same city as her rapist. It doesn't matter how we come before God with praise. The important thing is that we do indeed praise him – for all that he has done, is doing and for all that he will do in using all kinds of situations and circumstances.

Jess Wilson, *The Cutting Edge*, Authentic Media, 2008

ReactionReactionReactionReaction

CIRCLE:

☺ ☹ 😐 •!• 😕 😮

TICK:

Total rubbish ☐   Not sure ☐   Worth thinking about ☐   Genius ☐

FILL:

....

....

....

....

Can You Tell Him How You Feel?

Helen talks

Have you ever been really honest with God? . . . I mean really?

It's easy to be honest with God when everything is great. You can thank him for his blessings and provision and that you are just walking in the sunshine of life! It's easy to praise him and thank him. But can you be honest with him when things aren't so good?

Whether or not you can really be honest with someone is usually a bit of a test of the strength of your relationship. I've got friends who I could give it to straight if something had gone wrong. I could tell them how I was feeling; I could shout or cry or rant and know that they would still be my friend the next day. I've also got friends who I wouldn't feel able to be that vulnerable with. I wouldn't be totally sure they would get what I was going through, or I would wonder if they would judge me or think I was weird for getting so upset.

The question is, **DO YOU THINK GOD CAN HANDLE YOU BEING HONEST** – and do you think your relationship with him is strong enough to handle it, especially if you want to rant at him, not just to him?

You might be going through stuff that makes you feel mad with God or think that he doesn't care. Sometimes you won't 'feel' like he loves you or like he is there or has a great plan for you. Chip and I have a friend who recently got out of prison after being wrongly accused and put away for 16 months. On top of that, his wife walked away from him and God, he lost his job, his home and pretty much everything else. His name has totally been cleared now and he is a free man and his attitude about the whole thing and his relationship with God is AMAZING! However, I'm sure he had some times in prison of saying, 'God, do you actually love me?' 'God are you even real?' 'God how can I possibly believe you have a good plan for my life if this is where I have ended up?'

We can't always understand God's plan or why things are hard, but we can be sure that God can handle us being honest with him. **WHAT HE WANTS IS A RELATIONSHIP WITH US**, and if we only ever talk to him when we feel good and we are happy with everything it will be a pretty lopsided relationship.

David, who God said was a man after his own heart, spent loads of time praising God but also shouting and complaining to God, telling him how he really felt, good or bad. In Psalm 13 he says:

```
How long will you forget me, LORD?
  Will you forget me forever?
  How long will you refuse to accept me?
How long must I wonder if you have forgotten me?
  How long must I feel this sadness in my heart?
  How long will my enemy win against me?
LORD my God, look at me and give me an answer.
  Make me feel strong again, or I will die.
```

I don't know how you like to speak to God but you could try getting alone and talking or shouting out loud. Try writing out your thoughts in a journal or going for a long prayer walk to talk things through with God in your head or out loud.

Remember that God will not validate himself through your feelings but he is interested in how you feel. Once you've got everything off your chest, think about reading through and declaring some of the verses in the following extract and declaring them over your life or your situation if appropriate.

ReactionReactionReactionReaction

CIRCLE:

TICK:

Total rubbish ☐   Not sure ☐   Worth thinking about ☐   Genius ☐

FILL:

....
....

Name: Johnny May

Age: 18

Town: Crewe

Occupation: Student

What are you studying?

A-levels in maths, physics and chemistry

What is the cruellest thing your brother/sister has ever done to you?

When I was little, he hung my favourite teddy with my school tie on my curtain rail. Very cruel!

What is the greatest gift your sibling has ever given you?

Laughter

What's the first song you ever learned?

'Jingle Bells'

What is your favourite smell?

A nice curry.

Do you know anyone who struggles with depression?

Yes

What are some practical ways you feel that you can help?

Buy them a cream egg.

Great! Anything else?

Pray for them.

Hope

'Be strong and brave. Don't be afraid of those people because the LORD your God is with you. He will not fail you or leave you.'
(Deuteronomy 31:6)

God has said,
'I will never leave you;
    I will never run away from you.'
(Hebrews 13:5)

Why am I so sad?
    Why am I so upset?
I tell myself, 'Wait for God's help!
    You will again be able to praise him,
    your God, the one who will save you.'
(Psalm 42:5)

Hope that is delayed makes you sad, but a wish that comes true fills you with joy.
(Proverbs 13:12)

'I have good plans for you. I don't plan to hurt you. I plan to give you hope and a good future. Then you will call my name. You will come to me and pray to me, and I will listen to you. You will search for me, and when you search for me with all your heart, you will find me. I will let you find me.' This message is from the LORD.
(Jeremiah 29:11–14)

But then I think about this, and I have hope:
We are still alive because
    the LORD's faithful love never ends.
Every morning he shows it in new ways!
    You are so very true and loyal!
I say to myself, 'The LORD is my God,
    and I trust him.'

(Lamentations 3:21–24)

They threw me alive into a pit
    and then threw stones at me.
Water came up over my head.
    I said to myself, 'I am finished.'
LORD, I called your name
    from the bottom of the pit.
You heard my voice.
    You didn't close your ears.
    You didn't refuse to rescue me.
You came to me on the day that I called out to you.
    You said to me, 'Don't be afraid.'
You defended me
    and brought me back to life.
LORD, you have seen my trouble.
    Now judge my case for me.

(Lamentations 3:53–59)

We have been made right with God because of our faith. So we
have peace with God through our Lord Jesus Christ. Through
our faith, Christ has brought us into that blessing of God's
grace that we now enjoy. And we are very happy because of the
hope we have of sharing God's glory. And we are also happy
with the troubles we have. Why are we happy with troubles?
Because we know that these troubles make us more patient.
And this patience is proof that we are strong. And this proof
gives us hope. And this hope will never disappoint us. We know
this because God has poured out his love to fill our hearts
through the Holy Spirit he gave us.

(Romans 5:1–5)

We know that everything God made has been waiting until now in pain like a woman ready to give birth to a child. Not only the world, but we also have been waiting with pain inside us. We have the Spirit as the first part of God's promise. So we are waiting for God to finish making us his own children. I mean we are waiting for our bodies to be made free. We were saved to have this hope. If we can see what we are waiting for, that is not really hope. People don't hope for something they already have. But we are hoping for something we don't have yet, and we are waiting for it patiently.

(Romans 8:22–25)

Hope

ReactionReactionReactionReaction

CIRCLE:

TICK:

Total rubbish ☐   Not sure ☐   Worth thinking about ☐   Genius ☐

FILL:

....
....
....
....

Forgiveness

The LORD is kind and merciful.
  He is patient and full of love.
He does not always criticize.
  He does not stay angry with us forever.
We sinned against him,
  but he didn't give us the punishment we deserved.
His love for his followers is as great
  as heaven is high above the earth.
And he has taken our sins
  as far away from us as the east is from the west.

(Psalm 103:8–12)

'If my people who are called by my name become humble and pray, and look to me for help, and turn away from their evil ways, I will hear them from heaven. I will forgive their sin and heal their land.'

(2 Chronicles 7:14)

'I tell you that her many sins are forgiven. This is clear, because she showed great love. People who are forgiven only a little will love only a little.'

Then Jesus said to her, 'Your sins are forgiven.'

The people sitting at the table began to think to themselves, 'Who does this man think he is? How can he forgive sins?'

Jesus said to the woman, 'Because you believed, you are saved from your sins. Go in peace.'

(Luke 7:47–50)

Are you having troubles? You should pray. Are you happy? You should sing. Are you sick? Ask the elders of the church to come and put oil on you in the name of the Lord and pray for you. If such a prayer is offered in faith, it will heal anyone who is sick. The Lord will heal them. And if they have sinned, he will forgive them.

So always confess to each other the wrong things you have done. Then pray for each other. Then God can heal you. Anyone who lives the way God wants can pray, and great things will happen.

(James 5:13–16)

ReactionReactionReactionReaction

CIRCLE:

TICK:

Total rubbish ☐   Not sure ☐   Worth thinking about ☐   Genius ☐

FILL:

....

....

....

....

Reality Check

AN EXERCISE IN FORGIVENESS

Do you feel unforgiven? Do you feel that no matter how hard you try, God isn't really very pleased with you?

Once God forgives, he forgives and forgets. (Someone once said that he throws the sin into the deepest part of the ocean, and then puts up a sign that says 'No Fishing'!) You don't have to persuade God to forgive you – you only have to ask, simply, once and once only. The forgiveness is there – it's just that you don't feel it. The real problem is that it's *you* who are not forgiving *yourself!*

So, simply ask God to forgive you for the things you have done wrong – both the things you are aware of and the things you aren't. Then tell him about the things you know are wrong, but that you find you can't give up. He understands. He doesn't ask for the impossible. He knows that you are tired, and that your mental resilience is low.

Now write down your prayer, simply. Something along the lines of:

Dear Lord,

Please forgive me for all the things I've done that I shouldn't – especially
....
and ....
Forgive me, too, for the things that I've done without realizing and those I've forgotten about. And please forgive me for the fact that so often I still want to do these very same things again.

Please give me the grace to accept forgiveness, and release me from the feeling that somehow I've got to earn forgiveness by trying harder. I ask for all this in Jesus' name.

Amen.

Fold it up and put it away carefully: pick a place where no one else will find it, and where you won't routinely come across it yourself. You should know that it's there – but no one else should see it. The idea is that neither you nor anybody else should ever look at it again.

When you are tempted (and I mean tempted) to go over and over your misdeeds – as many depressed people do – remember the piece of paper. You meant it when you wrote it. That paper is a testimony to the fact that you meant it. Every sin that happened before you wrote on that piece of paper is now dead, buried and paid for. There is no question that it's gone, and you have the piece of paper to prove it – not that you need to look at it. All you have to do is discipline yourself to remember that you have been forgiven and that reviewing your past sins is not appropriate any more – in fact, under the circumstances, ruminating on your past (forgiven) misdeeds is in itself sinful, because it means that you are doubting that God has forgiven you. Consciously think of other things. And start to accept forgiveness.

When Jesus said, 'Love your neighbour as yourself', he also implied, 'Love yourself'. Would you treat your Christian neighbour as you treat yourself? No, you wouldn't. So learn to love yourself, to look after yourself, to forgive yourself. It's what being a Christian is all about. As the saying goes, 'Charity begins at home'!

John Lockley, ***A Practical Workbook for the Depressed Christian***, **Authentic Media, 2002**

Getting Help

Lord, don't leave me.
My God, stay close to me.
Come quickly and help me.
My Lord, you are the one who saves me.

(Psalm 38:21–22)

4

First up

Obviously, we hope you've already found something helpful in this book. However, to finish off we've compiled a ton of really useful excerpts to help you find the answers you need. We've dug out practical advice and suggestions from some of the best books around on this subject. So get ready to dive right in!

Always remember that, ultimately, God is our unending source of help in times of need. He provides for us and sustains us so that we can live our lives to the max! (John 10:10.) Live the story God has written for you. It's bound to be epic because he's a great storyteller. At times it may be tempting to moan and complain, but it's in these moments that we should determine to raise our voices in praise and thanksgiving to our King.

Let's keep the faith. Let's run our race with perseverance, right to the very end (see Hebrews 12:1). After all, if our hope is in Christ then help is just around the corner!

The POWER of PRAYER

'The truth is, you can say to this mountain, "Go, mountain, fall into the sea." And if you have no doubts in your mind and believe that what you say will happen, then God will do it for you. So I tell you to ask for what you want in prayer. And if you believe that you have received those things, then they will be yours.'

(Mark 11:23–24)

Prayer means being able to have a conversation with the most powerful being there ever has been, and ever will be. James 5:13–18 states that prayer is a fundamental part of our spiritual lives. We don't all need to be intercessors, but we are all called to pray – it's not just an activity for the 'super holy'. Prayer is an ordinary thing. We find God in normal, everyday life. God wants to weave himself into our daily routine. It can be so easy to put prayer off, so it's far better to take five minutes now rather than saying, 'I'll do it later'.

We often ask God for help in times of trouble and God delights in us asking – which is wonderful. God doesn't listen to us on the basis of what *we've* done or who *we* are, he listens to us on the basis of who *he is* and what *Jesus* has done for us. **BUT WE ALSO NEED TO TUNE IN TO GOD AND TALK TO HIM ABOUT THE THINGS THAT ARE ON HIS HEART**. We sometimes pray only about what's bothering us and forget to listen to God. Although God loves hearing about what's going on with us at the moment, he doesn't want us to ignore his feelings either. It would be like calling a friend for a chat, not even asking how he or she was, but just diving straight in to what our problems were, talking non-stop for an hour, and then saying, 'Actually, I don't have time to ask how you are. Bye.' Praying is like a conversation with a friend – we need to remember to listen as well as talking!

Forgiveness is a condition for having our prayers answered. We often expect God to answer our prayers when we have not come before him to confess our own sins.

- **We need to put our faith and trust in him.**
- **We need to confess our sins to God.**
- **We need to move away from habits of doubting.**
- **We need to obey the Holy Spirit immediately.**
- **We need to acknowledge Jesus as our Lord constantly.**

Jess Wilson, *The Cutting Edge*, Authentic Media, 2008

ReactionReactionReactionReaction

CIRCLE:

😊 😦 😐 😮 😕 😲

TICK:

Total rubbish ☐   Not sure ☐   Worth thinking about ☐   Genius ☐

FILL:

....
....
....
....

Talking Therapies

Some of us may feel that we are failures because we're unable to deal with our own problems, and that by admitting this weakness we are letting ourselves and our loved ones down. But actually, admitting that you cannot cope alone is one of the most courageous things that anyone can do. Acknowledging that there is a problem that you cannot solve alone and actively doing something about it is a step towards fixing it. It is well worth any shame or embarrassment you might feel in admitting it.

A dmitting I needed help was one of the hardest things I have ever done, but I would do it all again if necessary, without hesitation. To obtain a full recovery, some kind of therapy is essential. Talking therapy treats the underlying causes of a problem, unlike drug therapy which usually just suppresses the symptoms. It is possible to achieve a certain amount of recovery without professional help, sometimes even a significant amount. **BUT WE ARE NOT MEANT TO DEAL WITH EVERYTHING ON OUR OWN**, and although friends and family can be an enormous support, they are often too emotionally involved in the situation.

A therapist or counsellor will be rational, will give you honest opinions and will have no emotional attachment to you. **THEY ARE TRAINED AND KNOW EXACTLY WHAT THEY ARE TALKING ABOUT.** Yours will not be the first case they have seen. Talking to a stranger about personal thoughts and feelings can sound very daunting, but I found talking to a therapist easier than talking to someone I knew. There are no connections, and they won't be even slightly shocked by what you are telling them. He or she will be someone that you will probably never see again. They are not there to judge you; they are simply there to help you in a professional capacity.

Build up the courage to accept assistance. Speak to your doctor who can refer you or, if you are still in school or college, speak to a teacher that you trust. Most schools have their own psychologist, and these people are employed for your benefit. All you need to do is overcome a little pride and simply ask.

Jess Wilson, *The Cutting Edge*, Authentic Media, 2008

ReactionReactionReactionReaction

CIRCLE:

😊 😟 😐 😮 😕 😲

TICK:

Total rubbish ☐   Not sure ☐   Worth thinking about ☐   Genius ☐

FILL:

....

....

....

....

Healing the Emotions

Even if you have got into the good habit of using your emotions for today, you may still need healing from the backlog of stored memories and emotions that were too hot to handle at the time you originally experienced them.

little bit of delving into the past may be necessary. There are two approaches, which can easily be combined. The first is, with appropriate counselling, to explore those memories which seem to be causing most trouble, and to uncover forgotten and 'hidden' memories of things that are too painful even to remember with regret. The second is to do the same thing, but with a Christian counsellor gifted in the 'healing of memories' – in which, through prayer and counselling, God reveals either to the patient or to the counsellor aspects of the situation that need attention. These hidden memories can then be brought to God in prayer, forgiveness can be requested (if appropriate) and then the memories handed across to him to deal with.

There is no reason why these two methods cannot be used in conjunction. God sometimes uses supernatural means to deliver healing and sometimes ordinary human means. (In passing, it's worth noting that **IF ALL HEALING WERE SUPPOSED TO BE SUPERNATURAL, THEN GOD WOULDN'T BE CALLING CHRISTIANS TO BE DOCTORS!** It is important to see the spiritual and the human methods of healing as being complementary, not opposites.)

Going back into the past is a region where psychoanalysis and psychotherapy come into their own. By unearthing sources of emotional crisis – times when emotions have been stored up because they have been too difficult to deal with – the therapist unearths the source of the patient's problems and in helping the patient to experience or re-experience those emotions, allows them to dissipate, as they should have done long ago. Good and careful psychotherapy can be of immense benefit here.

You can do your own counselling on yourself, you know! If you start to feel a particular (usually unpleasant) emotion for no obvious reason, ask yourself why you should feel that emotion at that particular time. Is it because of your circumstances, or because somebody has reminded you by thought, word or deed of something that was unpleasant or saddening or difficult to cope with in the past? You can establish a routine of questions to ask yourself. What is it that makes you feel like this? What does it make you want to do? What does it make you think of? What events in your life spring most quickly to mind? These may give you a clue as to the source of your emotions.

If you're feeling panicky, why are you feeling panicky? Is it because you're on your own? What does being on your own mean to you – being left by your parents, being lost in a crowd when you thought you'd never get them back, being shut up in a cupboard by mistake (or on purpose), being friendless, being bullied, feeling left alone by God as well as by man? Explore your feelings, explore your memories, explore the connections that you find developing. It may help you to go into a quiet room where you won't be overheard, and act out some of the memories again, just to see what happens, and what further memories it unlocks.

If you find that there are a number or recurring themes, then try to work out where those recurring themes come from – you may need to have the help of a doctor, psychotherapist or counsellor, particularly if the connections are not that obvious.

Finally, a word about healing of the emotions and the Christian. It should go without saying that God is God of the whole universe and quite capable of healing things that are in the far distant past, of forgiving them, and of forgetting them. If he forgets them, who are you to remember them? If, on your travels back through your emotions and through your own personal history, you come across things that you wish to God (literally) had never happened, then tell him! If they have bothered you for such a long time they must be very emotional, very worrying, very guilt-making subjects. Approach them, grab hold of them firmly with both hands, bring them to God – then open your hands and let them go. He is quite big enough. He is quite capable enough. He is quite competent enough to forgive you for them. There is nothing that he cannot forgive. **THE ONLY REQUIREMENT FOR BEING FORGIVEN IS THAT YOU'RE SORRY!** The fact that you have been scared to approach the problem for so many years means that you are desperately sorry for what happened, to the extent that you can't cope with it at all. There should be no question under those circumstances of not approaching God in the right manner! So go to him, tell him about them, and then let go. Having asked for forgiveness, ask also for the grace to be able to accept the forgiveness that God willingly and freely gives you.

John Lockley, *A Practical Workbook for the Depressed Christian*, Authentic Media, 2002

ReactionReactionReactionReaction

CIRCLE:

TICK:

Total rubbish ☐   Not sure ☐   Worth thinking about ☐   Genius ☐

FILL:

....

....

....

....

Spiritual Attack

When Christians are at work for God, the devil tries to get in on the act, but he is not bothered about Christians who are not a threat to him. In fact they make his life easy. They do his job for him, making the church seem irrelevant, out of touch, pointless, or constantly fighting with itself.

The devil attacks moving targets – those who threaten his limited power. Have you noticed that when you are trying to be obedient to God, or start praying more, or get involved with some evangelism, life seems to become more difficult? The devil will use illness, problems appearing out of nowhere, disagreements and arguments with people we love, anything he can, to distract you from being the person God wants you to be. God wants us all to be aware of what the devil is capable of, so that we can prepare for attack. But God wants you to remember that if you are a Christian the Holy Spirit lives in you. And he is greater than the devil (see 1 John 4:4).

What sort of things does the devil do?

The devil longs to whisper his destructive lies to us. He loves to sow doubt that God is in control of our lives. He tries to make people worship things other than God – even without knowing it. Pride is one of the traps he likes to use. Remember it's the whole reason he fell, because he realized that he was a model of perfection and beauty.

THE BIBLE CALLS THE DEVIL 'THE LIAR' AND 'THE ACCUSER' (see John 8:44 and Revelation 12:10–11). He cannot tell the truth and his untruth varies from subtle deception to full-blown lies. We can be free of his power, but we need God's help.

People laugh at me because I get scared by the most unscary films. Even the music in a remotely scary film can have me in bits! But I have learnt that this is God's way of protecting my head and ensuring that my memories and what I dwell on are pure and innocent. People also think it's odd that I am offended by certain types of TV. Even my Christian friends think it's a bit sweet and eccentric that I can't watch certain things. But I have to go with my own inner conscience and stick to the things I know are important for me. There are some things that disrupt my peace, give me ungodly thoughts or bad dreams. These are the things that I am careful to avoid. – Ems

> Brothers and sisters, continue to think about what is good and worthy of praise. Think about what is true and honourable and right and pure and beautiful and respected.

(Philippians 4:8)

If we fill our minds with the sewage of some modern-day films, this will begin to affect our hearts and attitudes. We will start to value the world in a similar way, unless we can filter it out and be aware of it. There may be films, TV programmes, computer games, books or magazines that you are filling your head with that you may need to rethink. Read that verse again from Philippians. Do they measure up to this test? If you are unsure, then **THE SAFEST THING TO DO IS NOT TO SPEND TIME IN THEIR COMPANY**. You have better stuff to fill your head with. Right?

When I was at university, some girls came and knocked at my bedroom door. They said that strange things had started happening in their bedroom and they were very scared. They weren't Christians but they knew I was. They asked me to go and pray in the room. As I went in, I could sense a coldness – as if a window was open. But it wasn't. They had described how appliances came on by themselves, even when they weren't plugged in. As I prayed, I didn't feel anything dramatic happen, but just a sense that God was now the biggest thing in the room. That was the end of their problems there. – Ems

In this situation something spiritual and unseen was happening. But as with all things that are spiritual – bad or good – they have consequences that we can feel and sometimes see.

When we are full of the Holy Spirit, even people who do not know us can often recognize something different about us. There is something special about being filled with 'Godness' that makes a physical difference to us.

We recently heard a story about a famous Christian pop singer whose gig attracted other young artists from the pop world. When asked why they were at the gig, they said, 'We love hanging out with this guy! The rest of the music industry is so dark, but he is just the opposite.'

These young pop stars weren't saying, 'This guy is just bursting with the love of the Lord.' They couldn't have known that, but they could see that there was a lightness about him that was attracting them to him.

So what do people meet when they meet you? Do they see someone full of light, or do they see someone tinged with darkness? There are people who are obviously full of bitterness and pain. Their faces and the way they speak and move show that they are hurt and damaged in some way. Maybe you feel a bit like this and the reason you feel it is because you have been doing things that are not healthy for your mind and body.

What or who is your God?

So what if you have dabbled in things of darkness – what should you do? The Bible is clear that **REPENTANCE IS THE FIRST STEP WHENEVER WE OFFEND GOD** – that's the first thing we should do. We need to put right what is wrong and put behind us all deeds of darkness. It's nearly always really helpful to talk and pray through all of these things with someone mature that we trust. If you have been affected by anything that you have read about here and want to learn how to leave it behind for good, please do something about it.

Ems Hancock and Ian Henderson, *Sorted*, Spring Harvest and Authentic Media, 2004

ReactionReactionReactionReaction

CIRCLE:

TICK:

Total rubbish ☐   Not sure ☐   Worth thinking about ☐   Genius ☐

FILL:

....

....

....

....

Angry with God?

Don't worry about getting angry with God. He understands. When faced with the situation outside the grave of Lazarus, Jesus himself wept. Why did he weep? He was about to raise him from the dead, so it couldn't be weeping for Lazarus. No, Jesus wept because of the damage and destruction that the devil and sin brought into the beautiful world God had made.

If you are angry with God about sickness or death, then your anger is misplaced. God is angry and sad about it too. He loathes the sin that makes the world the way it is, but he still loves the sinner. In the same way, when you are faced with death or decay, make sure that you are angry with the right thing. By all means be cross about the sin that ultimately is the root cause of the unhappiness and evil that has come into your surroundings – but try and avoid blaming God for it, because it isn't his fault! (Why God has allowed something unpleasant to happen to you is of course a different problem, and one that I haven't got space to go into here. If you need help in this area try reading *The Problem of Pain* by C.S. Lewis.)

So what do you do in these circumstances? Just get angry? Yes. By all means be angry with the sin itself, the sin that brought the world to its knees. Focus your anger onto that, onto the right place, and you will find, again, that being truthful is a very refreshing experience. **TAKE GOD'S SIDE IN BEING ANGRY ABOUT THE EVIL ITSELF**.

When confronted with an overwhelmingly intense problem, where sadness, anger and despair are very immediate, even when you have logically traced the source of the situation to the right person (i.e. the devil) you may still be left with physical feelings of intense emotion and anger. To help relieve these feelings, try exercise – the more exhausting the better . . . Stress and anger are often dissipated quite well by this sort of activity.

John Lockley, *A Practical Workbook for the Depressed Christian*, Authentic Media, 2002

ReactionReactionReactionReaction

CIRCLE:

TICK:

Total rubbish ☐   Not sure ☐   Worth thinking about ☐   Genius ☐

FILL:

....

....

....

....

Name: **Stevie Johnson**

Age: **16**

Town: **Nantwich**

Occupation: **Student**

What would you like to study at university?

English

If you had to live your whole life without a part of your body, what would you choose?

My left thumb. Or my nose.

What's the most annoying thing about having siblings?

Them! They're annoying.

What's the best thing about having siblings?

You don't get lonely.

How would you define suffering?

That's hard. Suffering is when someone is in pain and they need someone to help them through it.

Who, in your opinion, suffers the most in this world?

Kids in Africa who lose their parents, and then the older ones have to look after their younger siblings.

You're Still God

Jess talks

A while ago, I was in a meeting at a well-known Christian conference and the speaker talked about faith and about God still being God, regardless. He handed out pieces of paper and asked us to think and pray about a situation that we were finding it hard to deal with and hand it over to God. He wanted us to write down the situation or problem on the piece of paper and end our sentence with: 'You're still God and I know that you're still here.'

At the time, I had gone only six weeks without cutting myself, had been promised therapy but didn't know whether I would actually receive any and didn't know what was going to happen. I don't really know how seriously I took the talk that day because I was so wrapped up in my own situation, but this is what I wrote: **'EVEN IF THE THERAPY DOESN'T WORK OUT – YOU'RE STILL GOD AND I KNOW THAT YOU'RE STILL HERE.'**

I have not cut myself, or even had an urge to, since that day six weeks before the conference. The therapy I was promised never came and I had to get help another way, but God was still God – and still is.

I want to encourage you to write your own 'You're still God' statements, to slowly hand over the situation and circumstances you find yourself in to God, and to have faith in him and his deliverance. I'm not saying

that by writing something down on a piece of paper your problems are going to be quickly and simply resolved. But from my experience, that simple task of pinpointing the issue and handing it over to God with faith and trust is enough to remind you time and time again that God is continually with you, at your side, his hand on your shoulder. **NO MATTER WHAT'S GOING ON, GOD IS A STEADY HOPE, A SOLID ROCK IN THE FACE OF UNCERTAINTY AND DOUBT.** It helped me greatly to hand the situation over to God and to accept his help. Despite all the support I'd had, and everything I'd done to try to help myself, until I wrote down my 'You're still God' statement I had not entirely handed over the situation to him and let go of the reins that I'd held on to for so long. But when I did, God was in control and it was from that moment that my recovery truly began.

Jess Wilson, *The Cutting Edge*, **Authentic Media, 2008**

ReactionReactionReactionReaction

CIRCLE:

😊 😞 😐 😯 🙂 😲

TICK:

Total rubbish ☐   Not sure ☐   Worth thinking about ☐   Genius ☐

FILL:

....
....
....
....

Getting God's Perspective

As a teenager, I set myself the very unrealistic goal of achieving straight A*s in my 13 GCSEs, and although I did incredibly well in my exams, I didn't quite attain the goal that I had set myself, and because of that I caused myself a lot of physical and emotional pain. I felt that I had not only let myself down, but also my family and my teachers. I did exactly the same thing with other exams. My relationships, talents and gifts came under the same harsh scrutiny until my life became quite literally one big unachievable goal.

et's take a look at what God has to say. What do these verses from the Bible tell us about feeling like a failure and how can we apply them to our lives?

My faithful love will never leave you. I will make peace with you, and it will never end.' The LORD who loves you said this.
(Isaiah 54:10)

God is telling us that his love for us will never change – there is nothing we can do that will make him love us any more or any less than he always has done – and that the peace that he brings will never be taken away from us either. In the context of failure, this verse can tell us that although we may feel like we have failed ourselves, failed others and maybe even that we have failed God himself, he does not look upon us as failures, **WE ARE STILL HIS CHILDREN AND HE STILL LOVES US UNCONDITIONALLY**. Sometimes we need to take a deep breath, stand back, take a long hard look at the situation, and ask ourselves why we feel as if we have failed and why it is so important to us. If God is not expecting us to achieve straight A*s then why are we expecting that of ourselves? We need to try and see the situation from God's perspective.

> I don't even trust my own judgement. I don't know of any wrong I have done, but that does not make me right. The Lord is the one who must decide if I have done well or not. So don't judge anyone now. The time for judging will be when the Lord comes. He will shine light on everything that is now hidden in darkness. He will make known the secret purposes of our hearts. Then the praise each person should get will come from God.

(1 Corinthians 4:3–5)

In this extract, Paul is writing to the people of Corinth and explaining that it is God who judges him and no one else – not even Paul himself. This is true for us also. So why do we judge ourselves? We need to gain God's perspective and to learn to be a little less harsh on ourselves. **GOD IS THE ONLY ONE WHO HAS THE RIGHT TO JUDGE US AND WE NEED TO REMEMBER THAT** and to stop ourselves when we feel like we are being self-critical and hard on ourselves and each other.

Jess Wilson, *The Cutting Edge***, Authentic Media, 2008**

ReactionReactionReactionReaction

CIRCLE:

TICK:

Total rubbish ☐   Not sure ☐   Worth thinking about ☐   Genius ☐

FILL:

....

....

....

....

Restoring Your First Love

We make so much effort to maintain the friendships we've established with our peers and colleagues, and yet so often we forget about maintaining the most important relationship of all – our relationship with our heavenly Father. Maybe you've never experienced the love of Jesus. Perhaps this is something you would like to consider? Is a relationship with Jesus something that you would love to have?

How often do we blame God for the way our lives seem so messed up and problematic? But if we took a step back and took a long hard look at the situation, would we be able to say that God was in actual fact at the centre of our lives and beings? Even if the answer to that question is no, there is good news. Unlike our friends, no matter how badly we've treated God, no matter how long we've ignored him, or how much we've abused and disobeyed him, **HE DOESN'T GO OFF AND FIND NEW PEOPLE TO HANG AROUND WITH.** He's right there, just waiting for us to say sorry so that he can be part of our life again.

Every day I'm realizing how much my relationship with God needs to be worked at. That's the thing though: you do have to work at it. I used to think it would just happen . . . and then I realized that there wouldn't be flashing lights and angels bringing me his messages. I realized that if I wanted to have a relationship with my creator then it wasn't going to be handed to me on a plate. I would have to sacrifice certain parts of my world life and give things up in order to deepen my relationship with him.

Many people think that God speaks to us with a big booming voice . . . and sometimes he might do, but often he speaks to us through a passage in the Bible, or when we're praying – which means that we have to actually read the Bible and pray in the first place. That might mean that we have to catch our favourite television show on E4+1 so we can pray when it's on E4, but God appreciates every second we spend with him. We're human and God doesn't expect us to be perfect. He knows that we'll make mistakes – it's inevitable. But there's a big difference between trying to change and live for God's glory, and living how we like because 'God loves us anyway'.

We need to engage with God in order to maintain our relationship with him. God made us unique and loves each of us unconditionally. Just like our family and friends, **GOD WANTS US TO TELL HIM ABOUT WHAT'S HAPPENING IN OUR LIVES – THE GOOD THINGS AS WELL AS THE BAD**. At times of desperation, one of the first things we think of doing is to pray to God for a miracle, but when everything is going to plan in our lives – when we pass those exams, find our perfect partner or land our dream job – we forget about him and put him to one side until the next time we are desperate and in need of his guidance and comfort. We cannot expect to have a relationship with him unless we put in the time, just as we would have to with any other relationship. It takes work and it takes time, but have you ever noticed that life often seems easier and happier when you are sharing it all with God?

We need to rekindle that passion and relight our fire with God. In a world that is busy 24 hours a day, 7 days a week, we need to take time out and just spend some quality one-to-one time with our loving Father. He wants that more than we could ever imagine.

Jess Wilson, *The Cutting Edge*, Authentic Media, 2008

Reaction Reaction Reaction Reaction

CIRCLE:

☺ ☹ 😐 😯 😕 😮

TICK:

Total rubbish ☐   Not sure ☐   Worth thinking about ☐   Genius ☐

FILL:

....

....

....

....

Pray

Dear Jesus, thank you so much for staying with me no matter what. You specialize in being close to the broken-hearted, and my life is yours. I find so much joy in your presence, and this joy is my strength to get through each day. Help me to trust in you and give me grace to pray for those who treat me unjustly. I love you so much, and my hope is in you.

In Jesus' name,

Amen.